GW01048760

Original title:
Our Share of Night

Editor: Theodor Taimla
Author: Anett Arumets
ISBN HARDBACK: 978-9916-756-44-7
ISBN PAPERBACK: 978-9916-756-45-4

Umbra's Harmony

In twilight's gentle embrace,
Shadows dance with grace.
Moonlight weaves a tapestry,
Winds hum a symphony.

Night blooms with silent lore,
Stars whisper tales once more.
In the stillness, find your peace,
Umbra's harmony, sweet release.

Whispers in the Twilight

Dusk settles with a sigh,
Painting hues across the sky.
Whispers drift on evening's breeze,
Voices of the ancient trees.

Time stands still in twilight's glow,
Secrets that the night will show.
Lost in whispers soft and light,
Dreams take flight in the twilight.

Echoes of the Dark

When daylight fades to black,
Echoes of the past come back.
Silent phantoms roam the night,
Guided by the absence of light.

In shadows deep, memories reside,
Secrets the darkness cannot hide.
Whispering winds and silent marks,
Tell stories in the echoes of the dark.

Starlit Conversations

Underneath the boundless sky,
Stars engage in silent cry.
Thoughts and dreams in cosmic dance,
A celestial, mystic trance.

Light-years span their whispered talk,
Timeless secrets as they walk.
In this stellar realm, we find,
Connections of a starlit mind.

Moonshadow Melodies

In the stillness of twilight's embrace,
The moon casts shadows, a tender trace.
Whispers of melodies softly arise,
Serenading the stars in the silent skies.

Night blooms with a silvery glow,
Dreams drift and gently flow.
Time pauses in a gentle dance,
Under the moon's enchanting trance.

Hearts beat to the lunar tune,
As love whispers beneath the moon.
Shadows waltz in rhythmic grace,
A celestial song in that sacred space.

Dusky Whispers

As the day succumbs to night,
Dusky whispers take their flight.
Softly speaking through the air,
Secrets shared beyond compare.

Twilight weaves its gentle tale,
Solemn, silent, without fail.
Hidden voices from ages past,
In dusk's embrace, forever cast.

Silent winds through treetops sway,
Carrying whispers far away.
Echoes of a forgotten lore,
In the dusk, forevermore.

Ethereal Shades

In the realm of ethereal shades,
Mystic light in twilight fades.
Ghostly hues in tender play,
Dancing softly, night's array.

Shadows whisper, softly glide,
In this realm where dreams reside.
Silent murmurs, unseen grace,
Embrace the night, in time's embrace.

Hearts find solace in this space,
A world apart, a gentle trace.
Ethereal shades, a tender glow,
In night's embrace forever flow.

Stardust Echoes

Stardust drifts through endless skies,
Carried on the wind's soft sighs.
Whispers of the cosmos' song,
Echoing where dreams belong.

Celestial bodies gently gleam,
In this vast, eternal dream.
Echoes of the stars' soft glow,
Guide us where the stardust flows.

Infinite tales in stardust spun,
Journeys written, every one.
Voices of the cosmos call,
In echoes of the night, enthrall.

Midnight Murmurs

In quiet corners, shadows play
Soft whispers of the night convey
Dreams that in the darkness glide
On moonlit beams, our thoughts reside

An owl calls from distant trees
We listen to the subtle breeze
Stars above, a glowing choir
Lighting up our hearts' desire

The midnight air, so cool and sweet
Echoes of the day retreat
Underneath the velvet skies
In midnight murmurs, truth lies

Twilight Reveries

As day melts into twilight's grace
Soft hues of dusk begin to trace
A canvas painted with farewell
Where dreams in gentle whispers dwell

The evening star winks from afar
Guiding wishes near and far
Silhouettes of trees now bow
To twilight's calm and silent vow

Embraced by night, we close our eyes
To twilight's soothing lullabies
In reveries we'll find our peace
As daylight's reign begins to cease

Cosmic Embrace

Beneath the sky's expansive dome
The cosmos calls us to roam
Galaxies in dazzling spin
Invite our wandering souls within

Nebulas of colors bright
Illuminate the endless night
In cosmic arms, we find our place
In the universe's vast embrace

Stars align in ancient tales
Where infinity prevails
In the silence of deep space
Feel the cosmic embrace

Nocturnal Serenade

Underneath the starry veil
A nocturnal symphony prevails
Crickets chirp their euphony
In the night's tranquility

The moon, a guardian serene
Watches o'er the midnight scene
Rivers soft in whispering flow
Sing the songs the night bestows

In this serenade of night
Every sound, a pure delight
Hearts attune to nature's song
In nocturnal serenade, belong

Night's Veiled Beauty

Stars alight in silent grace,
Soft whispers in the dark embrace.
Moonlight paints a silver hue,
Upon the world in somber blue.

Shadows dance in midnight's calm,
A lullaby, a soothing psalm.
The night whispers, secrets kept,
In dreams where promises are swept.

Owl's call through twilight air,
Mysteries hidden, silent prayer.
Velvet skies in ebony,
Guard the night's veiled beauty free.

Silent Nocturne

Crickets hum their nightly song,
Notes that weave forgotten clong.
Underneath the sky so vast,
Echoes of the night repast.

Stillness wraps the world asleep,
In its arms, the dark runs deep.
Moon climbs high, a guardian light,
Watchful through the silent night.

Stars align in patterns old,
Stories of the night retold.
In the hush, the heart finds peace,
Silent nocturne, sweet release.

Nocturnal Elegy

Darkened veil, the night descends,
In its fold, the sorrow mends.
Whispers drift on twilight breeze,
Mourning sung through silent trees.

Midnight's cloak, a somber shade,
Wraps the dreams that once betrayed.
Silent tear on cheek so pale,
Nocturnal elegy we hail.

Stars will mourn with tender light,
Eclipsing all the worldly plight.
In the hush, we find reprieve,
A solace for the hearts that grieve.

The Night's Canvas

In the night, the stars will gleam,
Brushstrokes of a painter's dream.
Moonlight spills on shadowed ground,
Silent art without a sound.

Midnight hues in shades of blue,
Spread across the skies anew.
Every star a gentle flare,
Crafted with the utmost care.

Soft the whispers of the dark,
Each a line, a fleeting mark.
Canvas of the night takes form,
In its beauty, hearts grow warm.

Whispers in the Gloaming

The evening breathes in hues serene,
Soft shadows drape the world obscene,
Through twilight mists where dreams convene,
Whispers softly, voices lean.

Glistening dewdrops kiss the earth,
In hushed nights, they find rebirth,
Stars ignite in distant mirth,
Secrets of the night give birth.

Forest paths where spirits tread,
Leaves of gold in twilight spread,
This tranquil hour, softly led,
By whispers in the gloaming shed.

The moon ascends, her silvery sheen,
Embracing hearts that softly glean,
In the gloaming, so serene,
Where the ethereal whispers lean.

Realm of Darkness

In the veil where shadows play,
Through the realm where echoes stay,
Darkness whispers, night and day,
Guiding souls that lose their way.

Cold winds carry silent cries,
As moonlight dances, sorrow flies,
Eclipsing stars in velvet skies,
Darkness shields from prying eyes.

Ancient woods, with secrets bound,
Mysteries in silence found,
In the realm where spirits sound,
Darkness reigns, yet none confound.

Underneath the twilight's dome,
Wanderers find a cryptic home,
In the dark where stirrings roam,
Shadows weave their endless tome.

Twilight's Aria

When day succumbs to twilight's grace,
A gentle song, a soft embrace,
Melodies in twilight's space,
Nature's choir, its sacred place.

Cicadas hum, a subtle tune,
Beneath the rise of silver moon,
Whispered notes in soft commune,
Twilight's aria begins too soon.

Tree-tops sway in rhythm grand,
Touched by breezes, forest fanned,
Harmony, the earth's command,
As twilight's songs by night are manned.

Eternal echoes, clear and light,
Through the deepening, approaching night,
Carrying dreams to endless height,
Twilight's aria, pure delight.

Eclipsed Moments

Between the moments, time stands still,
An eclipse of joy, a fleeting thrill,
Transient hearts in silence fill,
Whispers lost yet linger still.

Shadowed secrets, softly framed,
Mysteries held, untamed, unnamed,
Through eclipsed moments, hearts inflamed,
In darkness, passions unproclaimed.

Glimmers of light, a subtle tease,
Time's illusions, with soft ease,
In the quiet, spirits please,
Moments paused, yet never freeze.

A dusk that lengths, night forgone,
In eclipsed moments, we belong,
Memories in whispers drawn,
Eclipsed, yet joy in night's dawn.

Echoes of Dusk

As twilight whispers, night's slim embrace,
Stars emerge to light the quiet space,
Beneath the trees, the shadows play,
The echoes of dusk, in soft array.

The world in shades of purple-hue,
Sunset blushes, the old and new,
Birds sing their parting lullaby,
As daylight fades and waves goodbye.

The coolness wraps the weary earth,
In this serene nocturnal birth,
Hushed winds tell tales of yesteryear,
As moon ascends, the dark is near.

In twilight's arms, dreams softly lie,
The whispers of the stars up high,
Nature's hymn, a gentle task,
In the echoes of dusk, we bask.

Spellbound Sky

A canopy of stars unfolds,
Infinite tales it gently holds,
Mystery woven in the night,
Under a spellbound sky's delight.

The moon, a beacon silver bright,
Guides the night with soothing light,
Constellations weave their lore,
An astral dance forevermore.

Gazers lost in wonder's gaze,
Through the vast celestial maze,
Dreams unfurl on cosmic wings,
In silent space, the universe sings.

The night a canvas, pure and wide,
Where whispered secrets softly hide,
Spellbound sky, a sight to see,
In your depths, we're wild and free.

The Midnight's Story

When the midnight hour strikes aglow,
Time stands still, the world moves slow,
Every shadow, every sound,
In the darkness, tales abound.

Moonlight spins its silver thread,
Woven in the dreams we've shed,
Whispers drift among the trees,
Carrying ancient mysteries.

Stars alight the inky sky,
Glimmers of ages passing by,
Each a keeper of a tale,
In their glow, behold the frail.

The night's embrace, a velvet shroud,
Clings to earth, fierce yet proud,
Listen close, and you'll uncover,
The midnight's story, like no other.

Chasing Shadows

Light and dark, the endless chase,
In every corner, every space,
Shadows whisper, shadows glide,
Where they lead, secrets reside.

Sunrise, the game begins anew,
Shapes emerge and shadows strew,
Through the day they twist and play,
Till sunset bids them all away.

By lantern's glow or moon's soft beam,
Shadows dance like in a dream,
Contours shift with silent grace,
In shadow lands, we find our place.

Life, it seems, a fleeting shade,
Chasing shadows as they fade,
In their depth, we see a spark,
Of who we are, both light and dark.

Moonlit Lane

Down the winding moonlit lane,
Whispers of the night explain.
Shadows dance in rhythmic cheer,
Stars above seem crystal clear.

Silver beams weave through the trees,
Night-borne whispers ride the breeze.
Crickets hum a lullaby,
While the sleepy owls nearby.

Footsteps gentle, soft, serene,
Echo through the nightly scene.
Mysterious and quietly grand,
Moonlit magic sweeps the land.

Time drifts by in silent grace,
On this path, our hearts embrace.
Every dream and every thought,
Like the moon, perfectly wrought.

Twilight Chronicles

Hues of purple paint the sky,
As the sun bids day goodbye.
Whispers of the evening's lore,
Unlock tales from days of yore.

Winds that murmur secrets old,
As the twilight world unfolds.
Lanterns flicker, lighting ways,
Through the dim and dusky haze.

Stars begin to softly gleam,
Life, it seems, a waking dream.
Silent stories softly told,
In this time of twilight gold.

Memories of days gone past,
In these twilight hues are cast.
Chronicles of joy and pain,
In the evening mist remain.

Stardust Symphony

Notes of silver in the air,
Stardust drifting everywhere.
Celestial tunes so softly play,
In the quiet night's ballet.

Galactic rhythms intertwine,
Forming melodies divine.
Planets hum in harmony,
Part of this vast symphony.

Meteor trails like violins,
Sing of cosmic origins.
Every star a quiet note,
In this universe so remote.

Symphony of stars and night,
Cradles earth in soft twilight.
Universe in perfect tune,
Veiled beneath the watchful moon.

Nocturnal Tales

Nighttime's veil, a story spun,
In the dark when day is done.
Moonlight casts its silver glow,
On the world that lies below.

Whispers of a thousand dreams,
Silent as the midnight streams.
Nocturnal tales the shadows tell,
In the night where secrets dwell.

Wolves sing high their ancient song,
To the moon they've known so long.
Owls with eyes like lanterns bright,
Guide the lost souls in the night.

Every night a canvas bare,
Stories painted in the air.
Nocturnal worlds unfold and gleam,
In the realm of midnight's dream.

Moon's Silent Vigil

In the stillness of the night,
The moon bestows its gentle light.
Beneath its glow, the world dreams,
Wrapped in silver, soft beams.

Silent guardian in the sky,
Watching over, ever high.
Calm and serene, it shines,
Marking time with luminous lines.

Whispers in the cool breeze,
Rustling through leaves of trees.
Shadows dance, shadows play,
Till the break of new day.

Stars gather in silent choir,
Moonlight fueling their fire.
Harmony in celestial space,
Moon leading with ancient grace.

Under its vigilant gaze,
Night's mysteries embrace.
Dreams unfurl in silent streams,
Bathed in the lunar beams.

Stars' Spangled Embrace

In the tapestry of night,
Stars weave stories bright.
Glittering in endless space,
In their spangled, vast embrace.

They pulse with a timeless glow,
Echoes from aeons ago.
Constellations guide our sight,
Through the endless, mystic night.

Each a beacon, a distant call,
In their radiance, we enthrall.
Infinite whispers of grace,
Adorning heaven's open face.

In their silent, twinkling might,
Dreams take wing, hearts take flight.
Eternal, timeless, pure delight,
The cosmos cradles us tonight.

Under their watchful eyes,
We find solace in the skies.
A celestial dance, a starry trace,
In their spangled, warm embrace.

Twilight's Last Echo

When day gives way to night,
Twilight casts its gentle light.
Softly fades the sun's glow,
Heralding night, just so.

Colors blend in serene hues,
Painting skies with soft blues.
Stars begin their nightly show,
In twilight's last echo.

Shadows stretch and intertwine,
Nature's lullaby so fine.
Whispers of the day below,
Kissed by twilight's soft flow.

Peace descends with each breath,
As day takes its gentle death.
Moonlight whispers, stars now grow,
In twilight's final echo.

Moments linger in this glow,
Time seems to move slow.
Night's embrace begins to show,
In twilight's tender echo.

Midnight Whispers

In the heart of night's embrace,
Midnight whispers, sets the pace.
Softly secrets start to flow,
Under moonlight's gentle glow.

Stars above in quiet might,
Illuminate the depths of night.
Silent tales they gently speak,
For those who care to seek.

Winds carry the night's refrain,
Through the stillness, a soft strain.
Nature's lullaby so clear,
Midnight whispers in our ear.

Dreams are born in shadowed mist,
Under night's heartfelt kiss.
Moments timeless, peace so near,
In those whispers we hold dear.

When the world is drowned in sleep,
Midnight whispers secrets keep.
In the silence, we're set free,
To dream in whispered melody.

Midnight Reflections

The moonlight casts a silver sheen,
Upon the ripples of the stream.
In silence, midnight thoughts convene,
Where shadows blend with whispered dream.

Stars above in quiet throng,
Wink secrets in their ancient code.
Here in night where we belong,
We find the peace from day's abode.

The whispers of the wind so soft,
Carry tales from distant lands.
In moonlit darkness, thoughts aloft,
We trace the path with unseen hands.

The night, it brings a tranquil sigh,
A gentle hush upon the scene.
With every breath, we wonder why,
In midnight's hold our souls gleam keen.

Glistening in the Gloom

A subtle shine within the night,
Where shadows drape the silent room.
Amid the darkness, sparks of light,
Are glistening gently in the gloom.

The dampened earth of autumn's touch,
Reveals the secrets of its past.
In twilight's hush, there is so much,
That in the dark begins to last.

By lamplight's glow the world is seen,
In softened lines, a tender sight.
The quiet whispers intervene,
And guide the heart through gentle night.

Raindrops cling to every leaf,
A diamond glint in nature's womb.
Through times of joy, through times of grief,
We're glistening always in the gloom.

Celestial Phantoms

Across the swath of velvet skies,
The phantoms dance in spectral light.
In silent flight, no one denies,
Their haunting beauty in the night.

They whisper tales of worlds unseen,
Of stars long gone, of dreams so vast.
Their silvery glow, a timeless sheen,
A glimpse of aeons long since past.

With every turn, they weave a thread,
In the grand tapestry of space.
Eternal echoes of the dead,
Their presence leaves a ghostly trace.

Yet even in their ghostly form,
They shine with life that never dies.
Celestial phantoms in the storm,
A wonder for our wandering eyes.

Black Velvet Horizon

A black velvet horizon drapes the dawn,
Where night and day in balance meet.
The world awakens with a yawn,
And shakes the dew from sleepy feet.

The edge of night, a silken seam,
Where stars and shadows softly blend.
In morning's light, we start to dream,
Of hopes and journeys with no end.

The dusky line against the sky,
A canvas for the morning's hue.
Across the void, our spirits fly,
To chase the garlands of the blue.

In twilight's grasp, we'll find our place,
Where velvet blacks become the morn.
Within this gentle, quiet space,
New dreams and futures are reborn.

Nocturne Narratives

Underneath the velvet skies,
Whispers of the world's disguise,
Stars unfold their silent sighs,
Tales beneath the moon arise.

Shadows dance on twilight's breath,
Guardians of night, we bequeath,
Mysteries of ancient depth,
In the realm of dreams, we weave.

Crickets sing their lullaby,
To the midnight's gentle sigh,
Stories float and amplify,
In the cool night's soft reply.

Lanterns flicker, shadows play,
Nighttime's secrets on display,
Whispered truths in bold array,
Until the dawn steals night away.

In the starlit stories spun,
Where the shadows gently run,
Midnight's tales are never done,
Waiting for the rise of sun.

Twinkling Confessions

Stars above, your light confide,
Secrets in the night reside,
Twinkling truths we cannot hide,
Beneath your gaze, horizons wide.

Silent whispers in the air,
Twinkling lights in spectacles rare,
Confessions borne without a care,
In the sky, beyond compare.

Glimmers in the twilight seam,
Echoes of a distant dream,
Illuminating through the gleam,
Confessions flow, a silver stream.

Underneath the cosmic light,
Dreams confess and dreams take flight,
Through the night, pure and bright,
In the starlit, sacred night.

In the silent moments found,
When the night is all around,
Twinkling truths without a sound,
In the starry sky, unbound.

Silvered Moments

Beneath the moon's soft silver hue,
Time's eternal weave breaks through,
Moments fleeting, dark and true,
Captured in the nightly view.

Silver threads of memories spun,
Softly through the shadows run,
Moments sparkle, one by one,
Underneath the celestial sun.

Flowing through the hands of time,
Silent whispers in the chime,
Silvered moments so sublime,
By the moon, a sacred rhyme.

Waves of light upon the shore,
Silvered secrets we adore,
Moments held forevermore,
In the night's enchanting score.

Beneath the moon's enchanting glow,
Silvered moments gently flow,
In the night's embrace we know,
Time's eternal, endless show.

Dusk to Dawn

Between the dusk and dawn, we find,
Moments fleeting, intertwined,
In the twilight, world confined,
By the day's and night's combined.

Shadows lengthen, softly creep,
In the dusk, our secrets keep,
Where the light and darkness sleep,
Promises in silence deep.

Through the night, a passage clear,
Guided by the midnight's steer,
From the dawn, the world draws near,
Mysteries in the stars appear.

Whispers carry through the night,
Dreams between the dark and light,
Till the dawn's first gleaming sight,
Ending dreams of endless night.

Dusk to dawn, the stories flow,
In the twilight's gentle glow,
Where the shadows softly grow,
Till the morning steals the show.

Celestial Harmony

Stars align in astral dance
Galaxies in sheer expanse
Nebulas in colors bright
Weaving through the endless night

Planets spin in perfect tune
Underneath the silver moon
Comets blaze their fleeting trail
In the void where silence hails

Harmony amongst the stars
In the cosmos near and far
Celestial spheres in radiant array
Guiding us through night and day

Shadows of Dusk

Sunsets cast their golden hue
Painting skies in every blue
Whispering the day's farewell
In the moments where shadows swell

Mountains draped in twilight's cloak
City lights begin to stoke
Veils of night drawn slowly nigh
As the last light bids goodbye

Twilight's bridge from day to night
Merging worlds in fading light
Whispers of the stars to come
In the silent twilight hum

Nocturnal Reflections

Moonbeams trace a silvery arc
Through the quiet, tranquil dark
Moments lost in thoughts profound
In the stillness, not a sound

Reflections in the midnight's muse
Silent dreams that softly fuse
With the whispers of the night
In the calm and gentle light

Stars above, so distant, bright
Casting magic in their flight
Embracing thoughts of yesteryears
In the depth of cosmic spheres

The Dark's Serenade

Whispers of the evening breeze
Through the rustling leaves of trees
Humming tunes of ancient lore
In the night forevermore

Melodies of time and space
Echoes in the night's embrace
Faintly sung by shadows tall
Answering the moon's soft call

Darkness writes its lullaby
Underneath the starlit sky
Serenade of dreams and sighs
In the quiet, midnight lies

Lunar Dreams

Upon the velvet sky, serene,
The moonlight casts a silver sheen,
Whispers of night, soft and keen,
Otherworldly, yet unseen.

Clouds drift by in silent streams,
Guiding thoughts to lunar dreams,
A cosmic dance in starry teams,
Echoes in celestial themes.

Shadows play on tranquil streams,
Moonbeams weave their gentle seams,
In slumbered peace, the heart redeems,
The soul's quest for ethereal dreams.

Stardust trails in nightly gleams,
Granting solace in moonlit beams,
Waking dawn with hopeful schemes,
From the realm of lunar dreams.

Midnight whispers, quiet reams,
Anchored by the moon's soft gleams,
In our hearts, the vision deems,
The endless flight of lunar dreams.

Gloom-Kissed Horizons

Beneath the dusk of twilight's span,
The horizon whispers nature's plan,
A somber glow, the night's began,
Gloom-kissed hues in twilight's van.

Twilight's veil, a darkened shroud,
Wraps the earth in silence proud,
Stars align behind a cloud,
In nature's lap, the world allowed.

Twilight fades, the moonlight glows,
Gloom-kissed paths the night bestows,
In shadows deep, where twilight goes,
A tranquil ebb, as daylight slows.

In the quiet, evening knows,
A gentle calm through night bestows,
Hopes and dreams in silence grows,
A peaceful hush that nature sows.

Beneath the stars, the night imparts,
A canvas dark for wistful hearts,
Gloom-kissed horizons, where dusk departs,
The whispers of the night, it starts.

Celestial Soliloquy

In the silence of the night,
A celestial dance takes flight,
Stars in patterns, pure delight,
Weaving through the darkened light.

Galaxies in whispered twirl,
Cosmic wonders to unfurl,
Secrets of the night to swirl,
As stardust dreams begin to curl.

In the sky's embrace so wide,
Planets in their orbits glide,
Celestial dreams will coincide,
With night's eternal, steady tide.

Nebulas in colors bright,
Whisper tales in starlit night,
A soliloquy of purest sight,
In the expanse of dark and light.

Cosmic echoes, soft and free,
A dance, a dream, a galaxy,
In night's own soliloquy,
We touch the stars, in silent spree.

Ethereal Eclipses

In shadows deep, the moon does hide,
Where sun and night in peace collide,
An ethereal dance, side by side,
Eclipses waltz with gentle pride.

Curtains of the stars unfold,
A cosmic tale both bright and bold,
In whispered lore the ancients told,
A dance of shadows, dark and gold.

Sunlight's aura, fades to grey,
Moonlight claims the fleeting day,
In this twilight, shadows play,
An ethereal ballet on display.

Celestial bodies intertwine,
In the heavens, they combine,
An ancient rhythm, so divine,
Eclipses weave their silent line.

In the sky's grand tapestry,
Ethereal eclipses, wild and free,
A cosmic waltz for all to see,
A dance through night's eternity.

Twilight's Palette

Hues of orange blend with night,
Brushstrokes fading into sight,
A canvas vast, the sky ignites,
Twilight whispers, soft delights.

Vivid strokes of purple hues,
Merge with dusk's eternal blues,
Nature's artistry ensues,
As day and night, their dance renews.

Softly fades the sun's embrace,
In twilight's terms, a fleeting chase,
Stars emerge, their light, a trace,
Of cosmic wonders, infinite grace.

Night's dark veil begins to drape,
Twilight's hues in shadows escape,
Memories in twilight's cape,
Endless stories, night does shape.

In the stillness, whispers blend,
Twilight's brush, the night amend,
Till dawn's first light, it will defend,
A masterpiece, both start and end.

Veil of Stars

A million twinkles, soft and bright,
In the velvet of the night,
Constellations, burning light,
Weaving tales of ancient might.

Galaxies and distant dreams,
Flow through endless cosmic streams,
In the silence, starlight beams,
Echoes of celestial themes.

Each star whispers stories old,
Legends in their light unfold,
A magic tapestry, pure gold,
In the cosmos' silent hold.

Shattered light across the sky,
Moments flash and then they fly,
In the stillness, shadows lie,
Underneath the stars on high.

Mysteries of night, profound,
In this veil, the secrets found,
Stars like diamonds, night's surround,
In their glow, the heart is bound.

A Night's Embrace

Night descends with tender grace,
Stars alight in velvet space,
Moonbeams soft, their gentle chase,
Wrap the world in night's embrace.

Whispers in the shadows play,
Mysteries of the dark display,
Dreams in silence find their way,
In the stillness, night holds sway.

Crickets sing in twilight's tune,
Underneath the watchful moon,
In the night, a calm cocoon,
Promises of morning soon.

Lovers' hearts beneath the stars,
Bound without the light's bright scars,
In the darkness, count the hours,
Moments shared in night's sweet showers.

Until the dawn breaks through at last,
Night's embrace will hold it fast,
In the quiet, shadows cast,
A night's promise, true and vast.

Whispers of the Dark

In the quiet of the night,
Whispers linger, soft and slight,
Tales of shadows, out of sight,
In the dark, a pure delight.

Silent murmurs on the breeze,
Nighttime's secrets, stars' release,
In the stillness, heart is at ease,
Voices carried through the trees.

Moonlight threads through shadow's weave,
In the dark, the soul believes,
Magic hidden, dreams retrieve,
Night's embrace, we never leave.

Soft caress of twilight's fold,
Mysteries in darkness told,
In the night, new worlds unfold,
Ancient stories, true and bold.

Whispers drift till morning's break,
In the dark, the spirits wake,
Nighttime's hand, gently take,
In its spell, the heart partake.

Silhouettes of Serenity

Whispers of the evening glow
Dance upon the twilight's flow
Silent shadows softly pass
In the veil of night's dark glass

Stars entice the dreaming sky
Glimmers where the shadows lie
Sculptured scenes of tranquil grace
Brush the moon's ethereal face

In this calm, the world suspends
Where serene night never ends
Softly drawn, these shades of peace
From the heavens, soul's release

Nature's breath in silence speaks
Through the hills and to the peaks
Illuminating paths unseen
In the still of night's serene

Harmony in shadows finds
Peace within the darkest minds
Silhouettes of calm and care
In the night, we're free to dare

Dreamweaver's Twilight

Twilight's fingers paint the sky
Mystic hues as day bids bye
Whispers carried on the breeze
Songs of night's enchanting tease

Crickets chirp and owls take flight
Guiding dreams into the night
Stars, as jewels in velvet lay
Tracing paths where visions stray

Beneath the twilight's tender ray
Dreams are spun where shadows play
Every wisp of evening's air
Weaves a tale beyond compare

Softly tread where night begins
Threads of dreams and silken spins
In this dusk, the dream we weave
Holds a world we dare believe

Twilight's kiss, a gentle guide
To the realms where dreams reside
A symphony of fading light
Dreamweaver's touch, pure delight

Midnight Mystique

Midnight whispers softly call
Through the darkened, quiet hall
Mysteries within its breath
Hidden tales, unknown depths

Stars like secrets in the night
Shimmer softly, silver light
Moonlight dances on the sea
Weaving midnight's mystery

Every shadow tells a tale
In the dark, where dreams prevail
Secrets of the midnight sky
Whisper as the world goes by

In this hour, truths unfold
Stories of the night are told
Beneath the cloak of darkened hue
Midnight's magic, ever true

In the silence, moments gleam
Lure us into midnight's dream
Mystique of night, so pure, so deep
In this charm, forever keep

Luminous Nighthawks

Nighthawks soar beneath the moon
Glowing with a radiant tune
Wings aflame with silver light
Guardians of the quiet night

Stars align and softly hum
To the beat of night's soft drum
Nighthawks gliding, spirits bright
In the peace of tranquil night

Glowing trails in darkened skies
Patterns drawn by unseen ties
Every flight a subtle mark
Painting visions in the dark

In the still, their grace unfolds
Luminous and fierce, yet bold
Echoes of their silent cry
Stir the dreams where shadows lie

Guardians of the twilight's glow
Through the night, they ebb and flow
Nighthawks dance with silent might
Guiding through the luminous night

Enchanted Evenings

Beneath a twilight sky so fair,
Whispers dance in the evening air,
Stars ignite like fireflies,
In this world, no one denies.

Moonlight spills on quiet streets,
Dreams awake as the night repeats,
Mysteries weave in the starlit dome,
In enchanted evenings, we roam.

Silhouettes of trees so grand,
Paint the canvas of this land,
Soft winds carry tales untold,
In whispers gentle, bold.

Hushed voices in the dark,
Speak of love's eternal spark,
Hearts connect with silent sighs,
Under enchanted evening skies.

Feel the magic, close your eyes,
Hear the ancient lullabies,
In this realm where time bends,
Enchanted evenings, our hearts mend.

Lunar Whispers

The moon speaks in silver tongue,
To the hearts, both old and young,
Waves of light across the bay,
In lunar whispers, come what may.

Through the veil of night's embrace,
Luminous beams gently trace,
The secrets of a world unseen,
Where dreams and reality convene.

Soft murmurs from the crescent's bow,
Guide the stars in their gentle flow,
Cosmic tales of days gone by,
Written in the night sky.

Listen close to her soft call,
As shadows on the earth do fall,
In lunar whispers, secrets keep,
Guarded by the night so deep.

Bathe in her celestial glow,
Feel the peace only night can bestow,
In the quiet, in the still,
Lunar whispers, hearts do fill.

Ephemeral Glow

Morning's kiss on dew-kissed leaves,
A fleeting glimpse, the heart believes,
In moments brief, a light will show,
Cherished in its ephemeral glow.

Sunrise paints the heavens bright,
Brief and pure, a stunning sight,
Whispers of a day's first breath,
Renewal felt in nature's depths.

Petals bloom, then swiftly fade,
In the dance of light and shade,
Life's beauty in a fragile frame,
Ephemeral glow in nature's name.

Moments pass on winds so slight,
Fleeting flashes pure and white,
In each sparkle, in each glint,
Life's transient, profound hint.

Treasure every fleeting light,
In dawn's early, tender bite,
For in the brief and swift hello,
Lives the charm of ephemeral glow.

Secretive Shadows

In the hush of twilight's veil,
Silent phantoms tell their tale,
Weaving through the dimming light,
In their world of secret night.

Whispers form in muted tones,
In the land where shadow roams,
Glimpses of the hidden past,
In shadows' hold, the spells are cast.

Cobblestones beneath soft feet,
Echoes where the dark paths meet,
Ghostly forms in moon's soft beams,
Dancing through forgotten dreams.

Curtains fall and shadows grow,
Mysterious and cool, they flow,
Guardians of tales untold,
In their silent, secret hold.

Embrace the shadows, close and deep,
In the nocturne, secrets keep,
In their arms so cool and vast,
Time's own refuge from the past.

Moonlight Secrets

Under the glow, whispers unfold,
Tales untold in night's cold.
Stars gaze down, secrets they hold,
Mysteries speak in silver and bold.

Shadows dance, a silent waltz,
Each step echoes, no one halts.
Crickets sing their hidden call,
Moonlight's secrets enthrall all.

Gentle breezes, whispers soft,
Carry dreams and lift them aloft.
Mystic hues paint the night,
Secrets bask in lunar light.

Whispers in the darkened air,
Ancient tales beyond compare.
In the calm, night whispers through,
Guiding light in secrets true.

In the hush, the whispers roam,
Moonlight guides them back home.
Night's embrace, secret's rest,
Under stars, they're at their best.

Shadowed Dreams

In the stillness, shadows play,
Dreams unfold in twilight's sway.
Figures dance where shadows lay,
Nighttime leads our minds astray.

Whispers of forgotten lore,
Echoes from a distant shore.
In the dark, dreams softly soar,
Through the night, forever more.

Mystic shapes in silent strides,
Where the midnight magic hides.
Dreams emerge as darkness guides,
In the realm where shadow bides.

Whispers weave through sleeping thoughts,
Bringing dreams that time forgot.
In the shadows, secrets sought,
Guide us to what dreams have brought.

In the calm where shadows greet,
Dreams and darkness softly meet.
In the night, the heart's heartbeat,
Finds its dreams, a shadowed suite.

Celestial Reflections

In the sky, reflections gleam,
Stars align where dreams convene.
Cosmic lights of silver beam,
In the night, a mirrored dream.

Planets spin in silent dance,
In their glow, our thoughts enhance.
Looking up, we find our chance,
In the stars, a timeless trance.

Galaxies in midnight's grace,
Reflect in dreams, a distant place.
Through the space, we find our trace,
In the cosmos' grand embrace.

In the quiet, starlight glows,
Guiding us as darkness flows.
Reflections in the night's repose,
Tell of tales that no one knows.

Celestial beams, a guiding hand,
Leading us through night's expanse.
Mirrors in the starlit sand,
Hold our dreams in night's command.

Nightfall Lullabies

As the sun dips out of view,
Night unveils a darker hue.
Softly sung, the night renews,
Lullabies in shadows' muse.

Crickets hum a gentle tune,
Underneath the watching moon.
Stars appear in quiet swoon,
Nightfall whispers, sleep comes soon.

Breeze caresses, soft and light,
Through the calm of tranquil night.
In the dark, the world in sight,
Lulled to dreams by muted light.

Hush now, let the night embrace,
Guide you to a peaceful place.
In its arms, feel the grace,
Of nightfall's sweet, tender face.

Close your eyes to starry skies,
Hear the softest, sweetest sighs.
In the night where silence lies,
Find your rest in lullabies.

Celestial Whispers

Stars above in silent thrall,
Send their whispers as they call.
In the night, they softly speak,
Mystic tales for those who seek.

Moonlight glows with gentle grace,
Silver beams on every face.
In the darkness, dreams ignite,
Guided by the cosmic light.

Planets dance in silent song,
Orbits weaving all night long.
Heavens chart their secret maps,
Time suspended in their lapse.

Shimmering Afterglow

Sun descends with fiery blaze,
Leaving trails in twilight haze.
Echoes of the day remain,
In the sky, a soft refrain.

Colors blend in hues so bright,
Caressing the coming night.
Shadows stretch and shadows grow,
In the evening's afterglow.

Whispers of the evening air,
Hold the warmth and day's affair.
Softly fades the light away,
Heralding the end of day.

Nocturnal Cadence

Night unfolds with gentle pace,
Stars align in soft embrace.
Melodies of dark descend,
Where the veiled and dreams blend.

Crickets sing in rhythmic tune,
Underneath the watching moon.
Every pulse and every beat,
Blends with earth beneath our feet.

Owls call in haunting cries,
As the darkness fills the skies.
Nocturnal whispers flow,
In a seamless, silent show.

Velvet Veil of Stars

Midnight drapes in velvet threads,
Scattering stars above our heads.
In the deep and tranquil night,
Glimmers soft and purest light.

Constellations mark the sky,
Ancient stories flying high.
Whispers of the cosmos grand,
Trace the tales with stardust hand.

Galaxies in silence spin,
Hid within the night's own skin.
Secrets held in twinkling sparks,
'Neath the night's enduring marks.

The Midnight Path

Beneath the moon's silvery gaze,
Shadows dance, and courage stays.
The path untrodden, mysterious and vast,
In whispered secrets, dawn is cast.

Silent footsteps on a trail unknown,
Among stars, where dreams are sown.
In darkness deep, the heart may find,
A guiding light, serene and kind.

Trees whisper tales of days gone by,
Leaves rustle in a lullaby.
Each step forward, bold and true,
Leads the spirit to what's new.

Through veils of night, onwards we tread,
By starlight's kiss, we are led.
Chasing moonbeams, fleeting and bright,
On the midnight path of endless night.

Symphony of Shadows

When evening falls, shadows play,
In silent symphony, they sway.
A concert of darkness, soft and pure,
Within the night, our hearts secure.

Whispers of the wind weave through trees,
Harmony in the rustling leaves.
Each shadow dances, a note so fine,
In nature's grand, eternal rhyme.

Moonlight drips in silver streams,
Casting light on midnight dreams.
A silent song, the night reveals,
In shadows, truth gently heals.

Beneath the stars, where shadows roam,
This symphony becomes our home.
In twilight's arms, the soul can soar,
Embracing darkness, finding more.

Twilight's Caress

Upon the edge of night and day,
Where twilight's breath begins to play.
A gentle touch, the sky's embrace,
Paints the world in hues of grace.

Whispered secrets in the breeze,
Carried through the dancing trees.
Twilight's caress, soft and light,
Bridges day and tranquil night.

Shadows stretch and softly blend,
As daylight slowly finds its end.
Twilight's golden, fleeting kiss,
Leaves the world in tender bliss.

In this hour of peaceful glow,
Every heart begins to slow.
Twilight's caress, so warm and mild,
Cradles night like a sleeping child.

The Hidden Hours

When silence reigns and time feels still,
The hidden hours, shadows fill.
A realm of dreams, both old and new,
Unseen by light, yet known by few.

Stars ignite the secret sky,
Whispers float as night hours fly.
In these moments, hearts entwine,
Bound by time, both yours and mine.

Night reveals what day conceals,
Truths we feel, that darkness seals.
In hidden hours, we come alive,
In shadows, pure and thoughts contrive.

The hidden hours, quiet and deep,
Where secrets rest, and souls may keep.
Here we find our whispered powers,
Within the night's own hidden hours.

Midnight's Requiem

In the still of night, shadows play,
Upon the walls, in dim array.
Echoes whisper, secrets old,
Midnight's tale, in silence told.

Stars alight, a timeless scroll,
Unfolding dreams, that roam and roll.
The moon, a guardian, soft and bright,
Watches over, the silent night.

Beneath the eaves, the wind does weave,
A lullaby, for hearts that grieve.
Softly, gently, a requiem sings,
For night-bestowed, forgotten things.

In the hush, where time suspends,
The world in shadow, finds amends.
Dreamers drift, on silent streams,
Embraced by midnight's whispered dreams.

Gossamer Nights

The night is spun of silken threads,
Gossamer fine, above our heads.
Stars like gems, in velvet laid,
A tapestry, by twilight made.

Moonlight dances, nimble feet,
Across the land, where shadows meet.
The quiet speaks, in hushed tones,
Of dreams and wishes, yet unknown.

Crickets chirp, a soft refrain,
Ode to nights, both wild and tame.
Beneath the canopy, of sky so wide,
Heartbeats sync, with the night's tide.

Breezes carry, whispers light,
Through the stillness, of the night.
In this realm, where dreams take flight,
Gossamer threads, weave pure delight.

The Twilight's Hold

In twilight's grasp, the day recedes,
A mellow hue, as light concedes.
The sky aflame, in colors bold,
Bids farewell, in twilight's hold.

Shadows stretch, and softly blend,
Dusk's embrace, as night descends.
The air is thick, with whispered lore,
Of yesterdays, and what's in store.

Owls awaken, in silence hoot,
Night unfurls, like a velvet suit.
The stars emerge, to guide the way,
Bathing all in their gentle sway.

In the cusp of dusk and dark,
Twilight leaves its soulful mark.
A time of peace, a gentle pause,
In twilight's hold, the world embarks.

The Dark's Repose

In the folds of night, peace descends,
A quiet hush, where time bends.
The dark enfolds, a sacred space,
Where shadows dance, with gentle grace.

Stars gleam soft, a celestial choir,
Guiding dreams, and hearts' desire.
The moon's soft glow, a tender kiss,
Brings solace, in the night's abyss.

Whispers ride, on midnight air,
Echoes of a world laid bare.
In this stillness, hearts find ease,
Night's embrace, a soothing breeze.

As morning waits, just out of sight,
In dark's repose, we find the light.
Softly cradled, by night's breath,
Renewed by dreams, that lie beneath.

Nocturnal Ambiance

The moon casts shadows on the land,
Enigmatic whispers in the night,
Stars like diamonds gently stand,
In the sky, so calm and bright.

Crickets sing their ancient song,
A serenade to night's embrace,
In the darkness, they belong,
Adding rhythm to this space.

Cool breeze whispers through the trees,
Leaves that shimmer in its wake,
Nature's breath, a constant seize,
In night's canvas all partake.

Quiet streams reflect the stars,
Ripples dance upon their face,
Mysteries of the world and Mars,
Engage in cosmic, silent race.

Nocturnal ambiance unfolds,
A tapestry of dreams and night,
Eternal tales, forever told,
In whispers of the soft moonlight.

Twilight Tranquility

The sky is painted hues of gold,
As the sun begins to fade,
Soft whispers of the twilight told,
In shadows that the dusk portrayed.

Birds sing their final evening song,
A melody to end the day,
Harmony they've carried long,
In twilight's tender, soft array.

Glimmers of the fading light,
Dance upon the gentle stream,
Creating moments pure and bright,
That linger like a fading dream.

The world prepares for night's embrace,
As twilight weaves its quiet spell,
A moment caught in time and space,
Where tranquil thoughts and peace do dwell.

Twilight tranquility descends,
A soothing balm for weary hearts,
In its gentle arms, peace sends,
A nightly song as day departs.

Velvet Aether

Softly draped in velvet black,
The sky unveils its starry cloak,
Nebulas in the void's track,
A cosmic ballet, firm and stoke.

Whispers of the cosmic dust,
Swirl within the astral sea,
In this galaxy, we trust,
Boundless realms of mystery.

Planets dance in silent flight,
Orbiting their distant suns,
In the stillness of the night,
Eternal ballet, never done.

Galaxies like swirling dreams,
Far beyond our earthly gaze,
Through the endless space, it seems,
Infinite in starry maze.

In velvet aether, dreams unfold,
Dimensions vast, a boundless oath,
Stories of the stars retold,
A universe that binds us both.

Midnight's Canvas

Midnight weaves a darkened veil,
Upon the world, a shadow cast,
In its stillness tales prevail,
Echoes from the ancient past.

Silver moon with gentle gleam,
Brushstrokes on the canvas night,
Weaves the fragments of a dream,
With its soft and tender light.

Starry constellations glow,
Patterns in the endless space,
Every twinkle seems to show,
Mysteries time cannot erase.

Owls hoot in distant calls,
Guardians of the midnight hour,
Down the starlit waterfall,
Falls the night's enchanting power.

Midnight's canvas, vast and true,
An artist's dream of endless scope,
Within its depths, a cosmic view,
Holding dreams and endless hope.

Galaxies Unveiled

In the velvet night's expanse,
Stars like whispers greet our glance,
Nebulae with hues so bright,
Guide us through the endless night.

Galaxies twirl in cosmic dance,
Mysteries that dreams enhance,
Dust and light weave stories old,
Of wonders unseen, untold.

Planets, moons in silent arcs,
Trace their paths through endless dark,
Alien skies that twist and shift,
In the cosmic spell they lift.

Through the void our minds explore,
Wonders of the starry lore,
Galaxies, a lavish stage,
Unveil secrets page by page.

In each twinkle, a story spanned,
In infinity, we understand,
The universe, a grand parade,
Of galaxies in light displayed.

Celestial Labyrinth

In the sky, a maze unfurls,
Stars as signposts, cosmic pearls,
Pathways twist through ethers vast,
To realms unknown, both slow and fast.

Galactic lanes and stardust ways,
Navigate through night and days,
Constellations carve the route,
In silence deep, we follow suit.

Comets streak through shadowed trails,
Leave a gleam where darkness pales,
Through the labyrinth's starry threads,
Mystery on which it treads.

Nebulas hide secret doors,
To spaces rich with ancient lores,
Each turn and spin, a winding tale,
Of cosmic ships that never sail.

Lost yet found within the stars,
Guided by a force that mars,
The Celestial Labyrinth's silent song,
Echoes through the universe's throng.

Beyond the Horizon

Where the ocean greets the sky,
Dreams ascend, and doubts do lie,
Beyond the line that sight can't trace,
Hope and fear in soft embrace.

Horizons stretch, yet never near,
Promises both bright and clear,
A whisper in each golden ray,
Bids us chase the distant day.

Worlds unknown yet calling out,
Reality cast into doubt,
Unseen lands where visions meet,
Where destiny and wanderers greet.

Guiding stars and twilight's beam,
Blend the real with the dream,
Journeys start where limits fade,
In the twilight's gentle shade.

Beyond the horizon, whispers say,
Adventure breathes with each fresh day,
With every dawn, a chance revealed,
A future bright, in fate concealed.

Night's Requiem

Twilight's breath, a calm descent,
Daylight's glow in silence spent,
Shadows stretch where light once lay,
Night's soft voice begins its sway.

Stars weep light in velvet skies,
Echoes of the day's goodbyes,
Moonlight casts her silver tune,
In the stillness, shadows swoon.

Silent arias through the air,
Night's own song, beyond compare,
Whispers of the darkened sea,
Cradle dreams in mystery.

Each heartbeat in the quiet deep,
Keeps the secrets night must keep,
Lullabies from ancient lore,
Ease our souls and hearts restore.

Night's Requiem, a gentle sigh,
A promise that the dawn is nigh,
In its embrace, rest assured,
As dreams and hopes are reoccurred.

Luminous Veil

In twilight's tender, golden fade,
The world transforms, secrets laid.
A veil of light, so soft, serene,
Unveils the night's enchanting scene.

Whispers soft through evening's breeze,
Carry tales from ancient trees.
Stars awaken in skies so pale,
Dancing behind the luminous veil.

Moonlight spills on silken shores,
Weaving dreams through heaven's doors.
A cosmic ballet, wild and frail,
Underneath the luminous veil.

Shadows play in silent grace,
Painting night with a wistful trace.
Lost in magic, wishes sail,
Upon the winds of the luminous veil.

In the calm of night we find,
Peace within our wandering mind.
Wrapped in quiet, without fail,
We dream beneath the luminous veil.

Velvet Hours

In the velvet hours of the night,
Shadows dance in moon's soft light.
Dreams unfurl with mystic power,
In the deep, sweet velvet hour.

Whispered secrets gently flow,
In the stillness, hearts do know.
Mysteries of the universe,
Unveil in soft, whispered verse.

Stars above, in silent gaze,
Guide us through the darkened maze.
Luring us with tender charm,
In night's embrace, safe and warm.

Each gentle breath, a lullaby,
Underneath the star-strewn sky.
Velvet hours, time stands still,
With a quiet, tender thrill.

In this calm, our souls restore,
Velvet hours, forevermore.
Wrapped in night, a loving shroud,
Serenity within the crowd.

Celestial Lull

Underneath the cosmic spread,
Where celestial dreams have led,
Stars sing softly, a silent call,
In the night's embrace, we fall.

Galaxies whisper ancient songs,
Of where our tender hearts belong.
Through the void, a tranquil pull,
Cradled in the celestial lull.

Beneath the heavens, dark and deep,
We find solace, dream we'll keep.
Stardust kisses, gentle, small,
In the quiet, feel them all.

Moonlit paths we tread on high,
Through the vast and endless sky.
In their glow, our hearts are full,
Guided by the celestial lull.

Sleep, dear soul, in soft night's veil,
Let the dreams of starlight sail.
Carry hope and love's sweet pull,
Within the calm of celestial lull.

Silent Starwatch

In the stillness, gaze above,
To the stars, a whispered love.
Silent nights, where dreams reside,
In the starwatch, hearts confide.

Each twinkle speaks a silent word,
In the quiet, they are heard.
Guiding us through night's expanse,
In their steady, timeless dance.

Echoes of the ages past,
In the starlight always cast,
Tell of dreams both old and new,
In the silent starwatch hue.

Time stands still in this bright sea,
Where our spirits wander free.
In the silence, we find grace,
Feeling stars' soft, warm embrace.

Throughout the night, our visions soar,
Until the dawn creeps evermore.
Silent starwatch, calm and bright,
Guide us through the velvet night.

Astral Tales

In skies where endless stories shine,
Galactic threads in space entwine.
The silence speaks of distant worlds,
Where cosmic dreams are far unfurled.

Nebulae like painted veils,
Whispering soft, astral tales.
Stars that twinkle, secrets keep,
In the boundless, endless deep.

Planets dance in astral flight,
Circling 'round the sun's bright light.
In their orbits, secrets gleam,
Threads of the eternal dream.

Comets streak with fiery trails,
Through the void, their beauty pales.
Leaving whispers in their wake,
Pathways for the heart to take.

Celestial realms, a night's embrace,
Guiding us through time and space.
The universe, an ancient book,
In its depths, we dare to look.

Velvet Darkness

Through the velvet cloak of night,
Whispers dance in soft moonlight.
Stars like diamonds, skies adorn,
In the dark, new dreams are born.

Shadows weave their mystic art,
Enshroud the night in every part.
A tranquil hush, a gentle sway,
Where night's own secrets softly play.

Midnight's veil, a silent friend,
Where whispered truths and dreams transcend.
Each heartbeat echoes as we tread,
In velvet dark, where paths are led.

Luna's glow, a soft caress,
Guides us through the night's finesse.
In her light, we find our way,
Through hidden realms of night and day.

Velvet darkness, calm and still,
Holds the world in quiet thrill.
A tender night's embracing kiss,
In whispered vows of silent bliss.

Nebulae Wishes

In nebulae where dreams are spun,
Colors blend as night's begun.
A canvas brushed by astral hands,
In cosmic hues where magic stands.

Whispers of the stars align,
Weaving wishes so divine.
Through the ether, silent calls,
In vast celestial halls.

Glistening clouds of stardust swirl,
Cradling dreams within their curl.
Each particle, a wish bestowed,
Glimmering in the night's abode.

Galaxies of endless light,
Harboring our hearts' delight.
In their glow, hope intertwines,
With wishes born, in cosmic lines.

Nebulae, where wishes soar,
Bound by dreams and so much more.
Through their depths, our spirits fly,
In the endless, starry sky.

Star-Kissed Whispers

Star-kissed whispers in the night,
Softly bear the heart's delight.
Tales of old and dreams anew,
In their glow, they softly grew.

Celestial beams in gentle streams,
Illuminate our midnight dreams.
Each twinkle tells a secret sweet,
In the dance where stars and wishes meet.

Upon the midnight's velvet sea,
Whispers float and wander free.
In their quiet, tender voice,
Hearts find reason to rejoice.

Galaxy's soft murmured tunes,
Echo in the silver moons.
Twinkling stars like lullabies,
Soothe the night with gentle sighs.

Star-kissed dreams, a lover's pledge,
Wrapped in timeless, cosmic edge.
Through the dark, they light the way,
To the break of dawn and day.

Glistening Gloom

In the silence of the night,
The shadows dance with moonlight's bloom,
A world concealed from sight,
In the realm of glistening gloom.

Whispers of forgotten dreams,
Echo through the darkened skies,
A solitude that gently gleams,
Where every hidden secret lies.

Ghostly figures softly glide,
Through the mist so pale and thin,
In this world where shadows bide,
Dark and bright, a silent twin.

A breeze that carries ancient tales,
Of sorrows past and joys renewed,
Through winding, haunted ghostly trails,
A somber peace that is pursued.

In this realm of night and shade,
Glistening gloom reigns supreme,
Beyond the fear of light betrayed,
Awaits the dawn's redeeming beam.

Veils of Twilight

The sun sets with a final glow,
Veils of twilight softly fall,
The evening sky begins to show,
A hush upon the world, enthrall.

Purple hues and crimson lace,
Spread across the fading light,
Day's departure, slow embrace,
Leads us gently into night.

Softly whispering through the air,
The shadows stretch and softly blend,
Nature pauses, quiet prayer,
As daylight meets its gentle end.

Stars awake from slumber deep,
To sprinkle light in midnight seas,
Dreams and darkness start to creep,
Among the whispering evening trees.

Veils of twilight, soft and thin,
Encircle night in tender hold,
A peaceful hush as night begins,
The world in mystery, unfolds.

The Night's Confessions

In the stillness of the night,
Murmurs float on starlit air,
Whispers born of purest light,
Secret truths laid gently bare.

The moon reflects a silver sheen,
Upon the quiet, sleeping earth,
Guarding dreams serene, unseen,
Giving hidden hopes new birth.

Vows of love and dreams of sorrow,
Shared in shadows, soft and deep,
Stories of a distant morrow,
Gently stirred in silent sleep.

Beneath the canopy so wide,
Hearts and souls reveal their fears,
In night's tender, gentle tide,
Draped in moonlit, glistening tears.

These confessions of the night,
Held in silence, soft, serene,
Bathe the world in tranquil light,
'Neath the moon's reflective sheen.

Starry Soliloquy

Beneath the cosmic canopy,
A single voice begins to rise,
In starry soliloquy,
A whisper 'neath the boundless skies.

The stars, they twinkle and they sing,
Their ancient songs of time and space,
Eternal tales that softly ring,
In the vast celestial grace.

With every glimmer, every gleam,
Fragments of a story told,
Of dreams and places yet unseen,
In constellations grand and bold.

The universe, in hushed reply,
Listens to the mystic voice,
In silent echoes from on high,
As heavens and the heart rejoice.

In starry soliloquy tonight,
The soul finds peace and voices heard,
Wrapped in the celestial light,
Revere the beauty of the word.

Evening's Embrace

The sun sinks low, its rays retreat
Stars arise, a glittering fleet
Soft whispers of the twilight breeze
Cradle the night with gentle ease

Homes alight with a golden hue
Darkness descends, the night's debut
Shadows dance in silent grace
Welcome to evening's warm embrace

The horizon wraps in velvet skies
Lost in the embrace of lovers' sighs
Owls awaken with a knowing stare
Evening whispers secrets rare

Moonlight bathes the earth in glow
Time extends, timeless flow
Evening's arms around us trace
A tender, calm, celestial grace

Quiet streets in peaceful night
Lamp posts flicker with soft light
Evening's shroud, a gentle lace
Holding us in this tranquil space

The Lull of Darkness

Night descends with whispered grace
Stars aligned in vast array
Moonlight dances, shadows chase
A tranquil end to the bustling day

Crickets sing their lullaby tunes
Underneath the pale, soft moons
Wind whispers through the leaf-clad trees
Night brings calm, a sweet release

Silver beams on dewy blades
Casting spells where twilight fades
Every rustle, every sigh
A mark of night that passes by

Children dream in slumber's hold
Blanketed in velvet fold
The stillness of time, a soft caress
Darkness brings its quiet bless

In the hush of midnight air
Find solace, free from worldly care
The lull of darkness gently sways
Ushering in new dreams, new ways

Cosmic Lullabies

Stars above, a lullaby sung
In cosmic tongues, all rhymes unsprung
Nebulas dance, a sight to see
In the cradle of infinity

Softly hums the Milky Way
In the quiet of the night's display
Planets spin in rhythmic sway
A celestial promise to all who pray

Comets scrawl their fleeting trace
Across the velvet's deep embrace
Galaxies whisper ancient tales
In cosmic lullabies, love prevails

Constellations in perfect form
Guide us through the cosmic storm
In their patterns, we find peace
Endless wonders, each a masterpiece

Night's embrace with starlit eyes
Soothing hearts with cosmic sighs
Sleep beneath the universe's gleam
Wrapped in dreams, a starlit theme

The Midnight Tapestry

Threads of night in darkened skies
Weave a tapestry with lunar dyes
Each star a stitch in heaven's seam
Midnight woven, a crafted dream

Clouds drift in a silent sweep
Guardians as the world does sleep
Shimmering threads of silver spun
In the tapestry, night's begun

Darkness drapes in velvet fold
Mysteries of the night unfold
Every glance, a hidden story
Midnight's canvas tells with glory

Auroras dance in vibrant hues
Adding colors to the darkened blues
In the weave of timeless art
Midnight's beauty plays its part

Whispers of the night's caress
Wrap the world in dream-filled dress
The midnight tapestry we lie beneath
In its calm embrace, find peace, find breath

Astral Horizons

Upon the canvas of the night,
Stars like whispers softly shine.
Infinite dreams take tranquil flight,
In realms beyond the human line.

Galaxies in their grand ballet,
Dancing light through cosmic time.
Mysteries unfold, never stray,
Silent tales, profound, sublime.

Nebulas bloom in hues divine,
Colors blend in astral seas.
Eons weave a vast design,
Ebbing with celestial ease.

Planets swirl in distant skies,
Orbits carved in endless grace.
Each a world where wonder lies,
A spectrum of the boundless space.

Comets blaze through silent nights,
Trails of brilliance in their wake.
Ephemeral their fleeting flights,
Memories that dreams will make.

Veiled in Moonbeams

Beneath the soft, ethereal glow,
The world in silvered whispers sleeps.
Shadows on a misty show,
Every secret moonlight keeps.

Trees beneath their lunar veil,
Whispering winds their leaves caress.
Night's soft songs from dusk prevail,
In silence, they confide and bless.

Rivers gleam with liquid light,
Flowing through the dreams of night.
Tides of time in quiet flight,
As moonbeams keep the dreams alight.

Flowers bloom in twilight's care,
Petals kissed by gentle gleam.
Nature breathes a tranquil prayer,
Lulled in an enchanted dream.

Mountains under starlit skies,
Stand as sentinels serene.
In their majesty, time flies,
Veiled in moonbeams' gentle sheen.

Enigmatic Twilight

When day surrenders to the dusk,
The sky ablaze with colors wide,
Mystery wears a twilight husk,
Secrets in the shadows hide.

Crickets sing their evening song,
Night begins its whispered tale.
Moments stretch and shadows long,
As the daylight starts to pale.

The horizon paints a fading light,
Glimmers of a world unseen.
Stars emerge, embrace the night,
Sparkling in a cosmic scene.

In the stillness, hearts align,
Dreams and hopes in twilight's gleam.
Souls entwine beyond the line,
Lost within the evening's dream.

Winds of memory softly play,
Through the hours of half-lit grace.
Twilight leads the night astray,
In its enigmatic embrace.

Celestial Confluence

At the meeting of the stars,
Where cosmos weaves its grand design.
Planets drift in spectral bars,
An endless dance, so intertwined.

Light and shadow, intertwined,
Galaxies embrace and part.
Orbital paths by fate designed,
Each a story, each a heart.

Nebulas with colors hue,
Every shade a cosmic thread.
Mysteries both old and new,
In the vast celestial bed.

Constellations mark the way,
Guiding spirits through the dark.
In their patterns, hope and sway,
Celestial paths leave their mark.

Wonders of the universe,
In the silent reach of time.
Every star a whispered verse,
Confluence in rhythm and rhyme.